Content

Introduction

Vowel
Consonant
Cheat Sheet
How to use this b

BASIC

NUMBER

DAY-TO-DAY

ACTIVITIES

ACTION

BONUS

Index
Maps

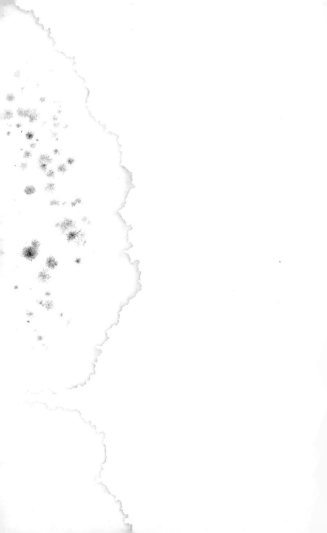

Introduction

Vowel Sounds

The following pages give examples on how to pronounce the vowel and consonant sounds in Mandarin Pinyin.

Following each are English and Mandarin sample words that produce a similar sound.

pinyin	English equivalent	Mandarin example
a (an)	sar (sun)	sà (san sang)
e (en, eng)	stir (forgotten/rung)	bě (ben,seng)
i (in, ing)	flee green sing (pin, reel)	bīng (gin ping)
i (after c, s or z)	bif	sí
i (after ch, sh, zh or r)	like th e r in purr!	chì
o (ong)	awe (wrong)	mō (jong)
u (un)	boo (one)	mǔ (xun)
u (and u after, j or x)	similar to dew pronounced with rounded lips	nū (qu)

Combination

Vowel/ Consonant combinations

pinyin	English equivalent	Mandarin example
ai	bike	bāi
ao	loud	pǎo
ei	lake	mèi
ia	mia	xiā
ian	yen	diān
iang	young	jiǎng
iao	meow	liǎo
ie	sierra	biē
iong	strong	qiōng
iu	yew	jiū
ou	toe	zhǒu
ua	guava	zhuā
uai	rye	kuǎi
uan	won	yùn
uan(after j, q, x or y)	when	yuān
uang	swung	kuāng
ue	you wet	xuè
ui	way	duī
uo	thaw	duō

Consonant

The consonants should be easy for you to get your
tongue around, as they'll all be familiar from english.

pinyin	English equivalent	Mandarin example
b	book	bàng
c	tsunami	cā
ch	cheese	chī
d	door	dī
f	food	dì
g	good	fèng
h	high	hǎi
j	jeep	jūn
k	kool	kē
l	love	lìn
m	moon	mǐn
n	no	néng
ng	sing	māng
p	pool	pēi
q	cheap	qù
r	rat	rì
s	sun	sì
sh	sharp	shào
t	tom	tū
w	wood	wāng
y	yes	yǒu
x	sheet	xiā
z	zero	zǐ
zh	gem	zhào

Cheat Sheet

In a hurry ? This may help you		
	Help!!	
	救命啊!!	
	Jiù Mìng Āh	

Thank you	谢谢	Xìe Xìe
How are you?	你好吗?	Nǐ Hǎo Mā?
How much?	多少钱?	Duō Shǎo Qián?
Cheaper?	便宜一点	Pían Yì Yì Dían
My Name is	我名叫	Wǒ Míng Jiào
How to go to?	怎样去	Zěn Yàng Qù
I want to go	我要去	Wǒ Yaò Qù
Yes / No	是/不是	Shì /Bú Shì
Want/ Don't want	要/不要	Yaò /Bú Yaò

Congratulations!

You have taken the **first step** in learning Chinese.In the next 23 minutes, you will **enjoy** learning Chinese in the **easiest way**.

Every Chinese word you learn is accompanied by English word and the Pronunciation.

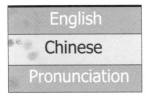

English
Chinese
Pronunciation

This book is **dedicated** to all those who wish to learn Chinese, in very short time.

At the end of each topic is accompanied by a practice.

	Let's Practice
	Very tired
	好累
	Hǎo Lèi

Introduction

5

Part 1
Basic

Pronunciation
When you learn to sing, you start with Do, Re, Me, Fa, So, La, Ti, and Do. Learning Chinese is much easier.

Imagine taking Opera singing lessons, There are only 4 vocal sounds to learn.

1

Sound No. 1
"Hā" (Flat Sound)
Don't open your
mouth too big

2

Sound No. 2
"Há" (Sound going
up a little)
Move your upper lip
a little higher

Pronunciation

3

Sound No. 3
"Hǎ" (Use your
voice from the
throat)
Sounds like some-
thing stuck in your
throat

4

Sound No. 4
"Hà" (Sounds the
highest of the 4)
Sounds surprised

Now, repeat the 4 sounds at 1 time, Hā, Há,
Hǎ, Hà. Repeat this practice for 9 times
before you continue.

Congratulations!

The intonation we learned above is known as
"Hàn Yǔ Pīn Yīn" Using Roman Characters to
learn Chinese is a piece of cake.

Pronunciation

One of the first thing I learned before visiting a new country is to pick up the language.

Some of the few words I will learned are, How are you ? I love you ? How much ? Can it be cheaper?

	Good Morning !
	早上好！
	Zǎo Shàng Hǎo

	Good Afternoon!
	下午好！
	Xià Wǔ Hǎo

Good Evening!

傍晚好！

Bàng Wǎn Hǎo

Good night !

晚上好！

Wǎn Shàng Hǎo

Goodbye!

再见！

Zài Jiàn!

Greeting

Marcus's Tip

Whether it is a job interview or a date, making the best first impression is always important.

My name is ___

我名叫 ___

Wǒ Míng Jiào___

Glad to see you

很高兴见到你

Hěn Gaó Xīng Jìan Dào Nǐ

Self-Introduction

Self-Introduction

	I work in ___
	我在___工作
	Wǒ Zài ___ Gōng Zuò
	I come from ___
	我来自_____
	Wǒ Lái Zì_____
	My hobby is ___
	我的爱好是___
	Wǒ Dē Ài Hào Shì___

	I
	我
	Wǒ
	You
	你
	Nǐ
	He/She
	他/她
	Tā

Self-Introduction

	Lonely
	孤独
	Gū Dú
	Tired
	累
	Lèi
	Let's Practice
	Very tired
	好累
	Hǎo Lèi

Self-Introduction

	Happy
	开心
	Kāi Xīn
	Sad
	不开心
	Bù Kāi Xīn
	Let's Practice
	Very Happy
	好开心
	Hǎo Kāi Xīn

Self-Introduction

16

A self-introduction is always a good start.

But, if you do not know how to ask questions, you may not get her phone number.

	What?
	什么
	Shén Me
	When?
	几时
	Jǐ Shí

Asking-Question

Marcus Tips

You may survive with only the 5 questions listed above in China.

To be more polite, you can start with:

May I ask___?

请问

QǐngWèn

Let's Practice

Where to go?

去哪里？

Qú Nǎ Lǐ

19

Can you imagine arriving at foreign airport where nobody speaks English?

To make matters worse, your friend is stuck in Traffic and is not able to arrive to pick you on time.

Now imagine that you do not have your friend's cell phone number.

So you decide to ask your way around.

Arrival @ Airport

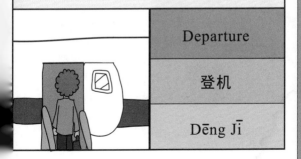

	Departure
	登机
	Dēng Jī

	Luggage
	行李
	Xíng Lǐ
	Dining
	吃饭
	Chī Fàn
	Arrival
	抵达
	Dǐ Dá

21

	Taxi
	出租车
	Chū Zū Chē
	Hotel
	酒店
	Jiǔ Diàn
	Let's Practice
	Call taxi
	叫出租车
	Jiào Chū Zū Chē

Arrival @ Airport

	Information Center
	询问处
	Xún Wèn Chù
	Toilet
	洗手间
	Xǐ Shǒu Jiān
	Please Bring me to
	请带我去__
	Qǐng Dài Wǒ Qù__

Part 2
Number

Learning numbers will enable you to talk about many things.

For example bargaining with the Chinese in the market, asking for the time and even discussing quantity.

1	一	Yī
2	二/两	Èr / Liǎng*
3	三	Sān
4	四	Sì
5	五	Wǔ
6	六	Liù

7	七	Qī
8	八	Bā
9	九	Jiǔ
10	十	Shí
100	一百	Yì Bǎi
1000	一千	Yì Qiān
10,000	一万	Yì Wàn
100,000	十万	Shì Wàn
1,000,000	一百万	Yì Bǎi Wàn

Numbers

10,000,000	一千万	Yì Qiān Wàn
100,000,000	一亿	Yì-Yì
1,000,000,000	十亿	Shí-Yì

	Let's Practice
	Lots of money
	很多钱
	Hěn Duó Qiàn
	Marcus Tips
	"Liang" is more commonly use in certain subject.

Money

27

Money is the root of all evil. But I guess it may be one of the most frequent words you will use in China when you are traveling.

How much? Can it be cheaper?
Too expensive! Discount please!

The 3 basic words you need to know:

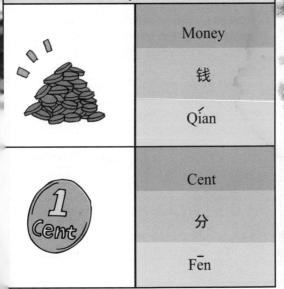

	Money
	钱
	Qían
	Cent
	分
	Fēn

Money

	Dollar
	块
	kuài

Remember when we learned about numbers in Minute 6? Apply that to the 3 words we learned above.

Example:
How should you say $5 dollars?

Repeat after me

$5= Wǔ (5) Kuài (Dollar) Qián (Money)

10 cent = Shí (10) Fēn (Cent) Qian (Money)

	**Price** 价格 Jià Gé
	**Discount** 打折 Dǎ Zhé
	**How Much** 多少钱 Duō Shǎo Qian

Money

30

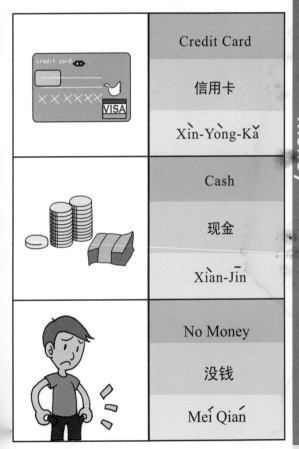

	Credit Card
	信用卡
	Xìn-Yòng-Kǎ
	Cash
	现金
	Xiàn-Jīn
	No Money
	没钱
	Méi Qián

Money

	Clock
	时钟
	Shí Zhōng

1 o'clock	一点	Yī Diǎn
2 o'clock	两点	Liáng Diǎn
3 o'clock	三点	Sān Diǎn
4 o'clock	四点	Sì Diǎn
5 o'clock	五点	Wǔ Diǎn
6 o'clock	六点	Liù Diǎn

7 o'clock	七点	Qī Diǎn
8 o'clock	八点	Bā Diǎn
9 o'clock	九点	Jiǔ Diǎn
10 o'clock	十点	Shí Diǎn
11 o'clock	十一点	Shí Yī Diǎn
12 o'clock	十二点	Shí Èr Diǎn
Second	秒	Miǎo
Minute	分钟	Fēn Zhōng
Hour	小时	Xǐao Shí
O'clock	点	Diǎn

Time

Time

	Morning
	早上
	Zǎo Shàng
	Noon
	中午
	Zhōng Wǔ
	Afternoon
	下午
	Xià Wǔ

Time

Time

	Evening
	傍晚
	Bàng Wǎn
	Night
	晚上
	Wǎn Shàng
	Mid-Night
	凌晨
	Líng Chén

The 4 Basic	
	Day
	天
	Tiān
	Week
	星期
	Xīng Qī
	Month
	月
	Yuè
	Year
	年
	Nián

Calendar

Calendar

Day		
Yesterday	昨天	Zuó Tiān
Today	今天	Jīn Tiān
Tomorrow	明天	Míng Tiān
Day after tomorrow	后天	Hòu Tiān
Week		
Monday	星期一	Xīng Qī Yī
Tuesday	星期二	Xīng Qī Èr
Wednesday	星期三	Xīng Qī Sān
Thursday	星期四	Xīng Qī Sì
Friday	星期五	Xīng Qī Wǔ
Saturday	星期六	Xīng Qī Liù
Sunday	星期天	Xīng Qī Tiān

ear

	Spring
	春天
	Chūn Tiān
	Summer
	夏天
	Xià Tiān
	Autumn
	秋天
	Qiū Tiān
	Winter
	冬天
	Dōng Tiān

Calendar

Month		
January	一月	Yī Yuè
February	二月	Èr Yuè
March	三月	Sān Yuè
April	四月	Sì Yuè
May	五月	Wǔ Yuè
June	六月	Liù Yuè
July	七月	Qī Yuè
August	八月	Bā Yuè
September	九月	Jiǔ Yuè
October	十月	Shí Yuè
November	十一月	Shí Yī Yuè
December	十二月	Shí Èr Yuè

Inviting guests to a banquet or dinner is part of life in China, whether or not it's business related. It is almost rude if you don't hold a banquet for your guest. Sometimes you invite your friend for a meal; sometimes your boss invites you for a talk; perhaps you will meet a lady you like and wish to invite her for a drink.

	Invite
	请
	Qǐng
	My Treat
	我请客
	Wǒ Qǐng Kè

	Breakfast 早餐 Zǎo Cān
	Lunch 午餐 Wǔ Cān
	Dinner 晚餐 Wǎn Cān

Invitations

	Supper
	夜宵
	Yè Xiāo
	Drink coffee
	喝咖啡
	Hē Kā Fēi
	Let's Practice
	Can I invite you for Breaskfast?
	我可以请你吃早餐吗?
	Wǒ Kě Yǐ Qǐng Nǐ Chī Zǎo Cān Ma

Part 3
Day-To-Day

This is an important chapter.

What if you accidentally meet someone in China?

Perhaps you will encounter someone who speaks Chinese in your own country.

Dating

Marcus's Tip

I have a friend from United States met his dream girl in China and got married in a week!

Dating

约会

Yuē Huì

What's your name?

你叫什么名字

Nǐ Jiào Shen Me Míng Zi?

Call me Mary

叫我玛丽

Jiào Wǒ Ma Li

How about you?

你呢?

Nǐ Ne?

Dating

Dating

Family

Father 爸爸 Bà Bà	Mother 妈妈 Mā Mā
Elder Brother 哥哥 Gē Gē	Elder Sister 姐姐 Jiě Jiě
Son 儿子 Ér Zi	Daughter 女儿 Nǚ Ér
Younger Brother 弟弟 Dì Dì	Younger Sister 妹妹 Mèi Mèi

Grandfather	Grandmother
祖父	祖母
Zǔ Fù	Zǔ Mǔ

Uncle	Aunt
舅舅	舅母
Jiù Jiù	Jiù Mǔ

Elder Cousin male	Elder Cousin female
表哥	表姐
Biǎo Gē	Biǎo Jiě

Younger Cousin male	Young Cousin female
表弟	表妹
Biǎo Dì	Biǎo Mèi

Family

	Horse Ridding
	骑马
	Qí-Mǎ
	Photography
	拍照
	Pái-Zhāo
	Drawing
	画画
	Huà Huà

Hobby

Hobby

	Dancing
	跳舞
	Tìao Wǔ
	Mountain Climbing
	爬山
	Pá Shān
	Watch Movies
	看电影
	Kàn Dìan Yǐng

	Reading 看书 Kàn Shū
	Drinking 喝酒 Hē Jiǔ
	Sleeping 睡觉 Shùi Jiào

Hobby

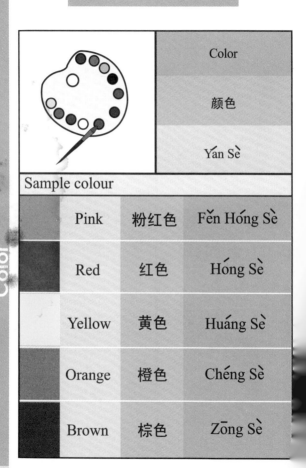

	Color
	颜色
	Yán Sè

Sample colour

	Pink	粉红色	Fěn Hóng Sè
	Red	红色	Hóng Sè
	Yellow	黄色	Huáng Sè
	Orange	橙色	Chéng Sè
	Brown	棕色	Zōng Sè

Color

Color

Green	青色	Qīng Sè
Blue	蓝色	Làn Sè
Purple	紫色	Zǐ Se
Black	黑色	Hēi Sè
White	白色	Bái Sè
Grey	灰色	Huī Sè

Let's Practice
White Skirt
白色裙子
Bái Sè Qún Zi

Sports

	Ping Pong
	乒乓
	Pīng Pāng
	Golf
	高尔夫
	Gāo Ěr Fū
	Tennis
	网球
	Wǎng Qíu

	Badminton 羽毛球 Yǔ Máo Qiú
	Soccer 足球 Zú Qiú
	Swimming 游泳 Yóu Yǒng

Sports

	Jogging
	跑步
	Pǎo Bù
	Volley Ball
	排球
	Pái Qiú
	Let's Practice
	Go jogging
	去跑步
	Qù Pǎo Bù

	Cycling 骑脚车 Qí Jiǎo Chē
	Skating 溜冰 Liū Bīng
	Martial Arts 武术 Wǔ Shù

Sports

Sports

	Judo 柔道 Róu Dào
	Taekwando 跆拳道 Tái Quán Dào
	Let's Practice Learn Judo 学柔道 Xué Róu Dào

Have you ever walked into a restaurant wanting to order some delicious Chinese food but have no idea how to order?

	Restaurant
	餐馆
	Cān Gǔan
	Waiter/Waitress
	服务员
	Fú Wù Yuàn

Restaurant

64

Restaurant

	Order
	点餐
	Diǎn Cān
	(Can pronounce like Chan)

	Menu
	菜单
	Cài Dān

	Bill please?
	买单
	Mǎi Dān

Restaurant

	Eat
	吃
	Chī
	Drink
	喝
	Hē˙
	(Sounds like her)
	Tasty
	好吃
	Hǎo Chī

	Cup 杯 Beī
	Tea 茶 Chá
	Alcohol 酒 Jiǔ

	Rice
	米饭
	Mǐ Fàn
	Main Course
	主食
	Zhǔ Shí
	Soup
	汤
	Tāng

Restaurant

Restaurant

	Special (House special)
	特色
	Tè Sè
	Dessert
	甜品
	Tián Pǐn
	Chopstick
	筷子
	Kùai Zi

Part 4
Activities

One thing you cannot avoid while visiting China is asking for directions.

Showing them your address or map, you may ask: would you please tell me how to get there? How far? Left or right? East or west?

Directions

	Asking for direction
	问路
	Wèn Lù
	How to go?
	怎样去___?
	Zěn Yàng Qù

KM?	**How far?** 多远? Duō Yuǎn?
	How long? 多久? Duō Jiǔ?
	Let's Practice Turn left 左转 Zuǒ Zhuǎn

Directions

Directions

⬆️	Up 上 Shàng
⬇️	Down 下 Xià
⬅️	Left 左 Zuǒ

	Right
	右
	Yòu
	Front
	前
	Qián
	Back
	后
	Hòu

Directions

	East
→‖➤ E	东
	Dōng
↓ S	South
	南
	Nán
W ◄‖←	West
	西
	Xī
N ↑‖	North
	北
	Běi

So, you are doing business in China or with Chinese. Some of the basic terms in a business meeting you may find useful to learn:

Signing a contract? I don't agree.
Yes/No. Do you have a proposal?

Meeting
开会
Kāi Hùi

Business Owner/Boss
老板
Lǎo Bǎn

	Manager
	经理
	Jīng Lǐ
	Employee
	员工
	Yuán Gōng
	Translator
	翻译员
	Fān Yì Yuán

Business Meeting

	Good
	好
	Hǎo

	Yes
	是
	Shì

	Agree
	我同意
	Wǒ Tóng yì

	No Good
	不好
	Bù hǎo
	No
	不
	Bù
	Don't agree
	不同意
	Bù Tóng Yì

Business Meeting

Business Meeting

	Signing Contract
	签合同
	Qiān Hé Tòng
	(He pronounce as Her)
	Partnership
	合作
	Hé Zùo
	Proposal
	方案
	Fāng Àn

Are you traveling to China on vacation?
Whether you are going alone or using a local agent, be prepared just in case of an emergency especially when you are not with a group.

Some of the common terms you may want to know include: I am looking for……a gift shop? Hotel? Map? Film? Or..I am lost!

Traveling

Sight Seeing

观光

Guán Gǔang

One day tour

一日游

Yí Rì Yóu

Traveling

	Tour Guide 导游 Dǎo Yóu
	Travel Agency 旅行社 Lǚ Xíng Shè
	Map 地图 Dì Tú

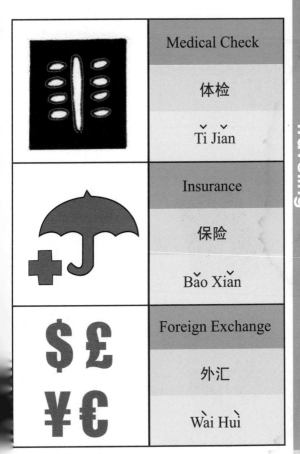

	Medical Check
	体检
	Tǐ Jiǎn
	Insurance
	保险
	Bǎo Xiǎn
	Foreign Exchange
	外汇
	Wài Huì

Traveling

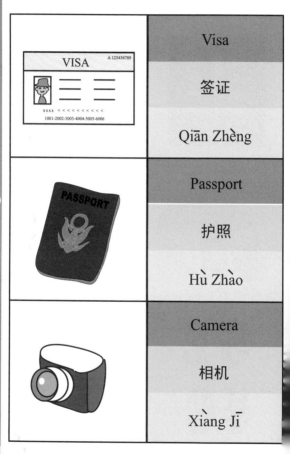

	Visa
	签证
	Qiān Zhèng
	Passport
	护照
	Hù Zhào
	Camera
	相机
	Xiàng Jī

	Air-ticket
	飞机票
	Fēi Jī Piào
	Scenic Spot
	风景区
	Fēng Jǐng Qū
	Gift Shop
	礼品店
	Lǐ Pǐn Diàn

Traveling

	Lost
	迷路
	Mí Lù
	Film
	胶卷
	Jiāo Juǎn
	Let's Practice
	I'm lost
	我迷路
	Wǒ Mí Lù

	Compass 指南针 Zhǐ Nán Zhēng
	Airplane 飞机 Fēi Jī
	Airport 飞机场 Fēi Jī Chǎng

Traveling

	Bar
	酒吧
	Jiǔ Bā
	Youth Hotel
	青年旅店
	Qīng Nián Lǚ Diàn
	Shopping
	购物
	Gòu Wù

Chinese products are good and inexpensive! Shopping in China can be a memorable experience.

What do you like to buy?
Fruit? Dresses? Jewelry ?

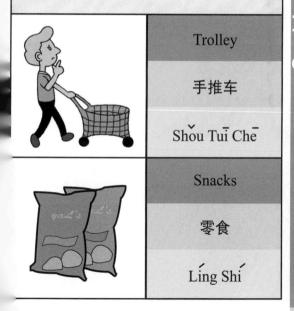

	Trolley
	手推车
	Shǒu Tuī Chē
	Snacks
	零食
	Líng Shí

	Fruit
	水果
	Shǔi Gǔo
	Vegetable
	蔬菜
	Shū Cài
	Meat
	肉
	Ròu

	Chicken 鸡 Jī
	Bread 面包 Miàn Bāo
	Biscuit 饼干 Bǐng Gān

	Office Stationary
	办公用品
	Bàn Gōng Yòng Pǐn
	Pen
	笔
	Bǐ
	Book
	书
	Shū

	Shampoo
	洗发水
	Xǐ Fà Shuǐ
	Soap
	肥皂
	Féi Zào
	Cosmetics
	化妆品
	Huà Zhuāng pǐn

Shopping

	Clothes
	衣服
	Yī Fú
	Dress
	裙子
	Qún Zi
	Sports Wear
	运动装
	Yùn Dòng Zhuāng

	Pants
	裤子
	Kù Zī
	Underwear
	内裤
	Nèi Kù
	Let's Practice
	Buy underwear
	买内裤
	Mǎi Nèi Kù

Shopping

Shopping

	Computer
	电脑
	Diàn Nǎo
	Electronics
	电子产品
	Diàn Zǐ Chǎn Pǐn
	Jewelry
	珠宝
	Zhū Bǎo

Whats your Occupation?

你的职业是什么?

Nǐ De Zhí Yè Shì Shen Me?

I am a____

我是____

Wǒ Shì____

Cook

厨师

Chú Shī

Occupations

98

	Teacher
	教师
	Jiào Shī
	Student
	学生
	Xué Shēng
	Let's Practice
	My teacher
	我的教师
	Wǒ De Jiào Shī

Occupations

	Driver
	司机
	Sī Jī
	Police
	警察
	Jǐng Chá
	Soldier
	军人
	Jūn Rén

Occupations

Occupations

	Maid
	佣人
	Yòng Rén
	Accountant
	会计师
	Kuài Jì Shī
	Let's Practice
	Police coming
	警察来了
	Jǐng Chá Lái Le

	Judge
	法官
	Fǎ Guān
	Lawyer
	律师
	Lǜ Shī
	Government Officer
	政府官员
	Zhèng Fǔ Guān Yuán

Occupations

	Doctor
	医生
	Yī Shēng
	Pharmacist
	药剂师
	Yào Jì Shī
	Nurse
	护士
	Hù Shì

Occupations

	Dentist 牙医 Yá Yī
	Business man 商人 Shāng Rén
	Singer 歌手 Gē Shǒu

Occupations

	Designer
	设计师
	Shè Jì Shī
	Artist
	艺术家
	Yì Shù Jiā
	Author
	作家
	Zuò Jiā

Model

模特

Mó Tè

Actor/Actress

演员

Yǎn Yuán

Let's Practice

Good actor

好演员

Hǎo Yǎn Yuán

Occupations

Occupations

	Stewardess
	空姐
	Kōng Jiě
	Nanny
	保姆
	Báo Mǔ
	Let's Practice
	I love Stewardess
	我爱空姐
	Wǒ Ài Kōng Jiě

Part 5
Action

At Home

	Home 家 Jiā
	House 屋子 Wū Zi
	Room 房间 Fáng Jiān

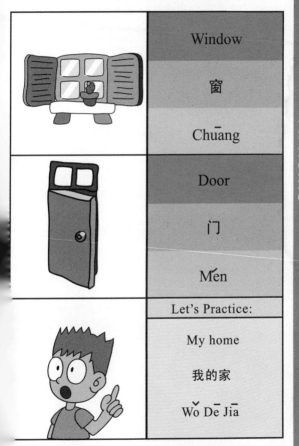

At Home

	Window
	窗
	Chuāng
	Door
	门
	Mén
	Let's Practice:
	My home
	我的家
	Wǒ De Jiā

At Home

	Swimming Pool 游泳池 Yóu Yǒng Chí
	Garden 花园 Huā Yuán
	Car 车 Chē

	Car Park
	停车库
	Tíng Chē Kù
	Table
	桌子
	Zhuō Zi
	Television
	电视机
	Diàn Shì Jī

At Home

At Home

	Main Hall
	大厅
	Dà Tīng
	Maid's Room
	佣人房
	Yòng Rén Fáng
	Carpet
	地毯
	Dì Tǎn

	Sofa
	沙发
	Shā Fā
	Guest Meeting Room
	会客厅
	Huì Kè Tīng
	Let's Practice
	Where is main hall?
	大厅在哪?
	Dà Tīng Zài Nǎ

At Home

At Home

	Store Room
	储藏室
	Chǔ Cáng Shì
	Dinning Table
	饭桌
	Fàn Zhuō
	Dinning Hall
	饭厅
	Fàn Tīng

Stairs

楼梯

Lóu Tī

Kitchen

厨房

Chú Fáng

Let's Practice

Where is kitchen?

厨房在哪?

Chú Fáng Zài Nǎ

At Home

At Home

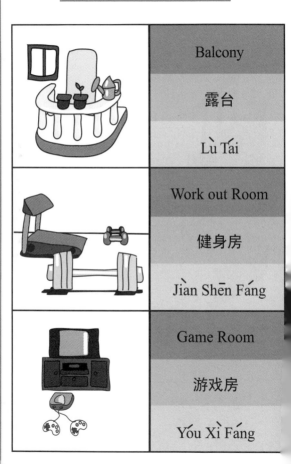

	Balcony
	露台
	Lù Tái
	Work out Room
	健身房
	Jìan Shēn Fáng
	Game Room
	游戏房
	Yóu Xì Fáng

	Study Room
	书房
	Shū Fáng
	Master Bed Room
	主人房
	Zhǔ Rén Fáng
	Bedroom
	睡房
	Shuì Fáng

At Home

118

At Home

	Baby Room
	婴儿房
	Yīng Ér Fáng
	Guest Room
	客人房
	Kè Rén Fáng
	Let's Practice
	Where is balcony?
	露台在哪？
	Lù Tái Zài Nǎ

Where you want to go?

	Have Fun
	享乐
	Xiǎng Lè
	Holiday
	度假
	Dù Jià
	Let's Practice
	Go gym
	去健身
	Qù Jiàn Shēn

	Theme Park
	游乐园
	Yóu Lè Yuán
	Rest
	休息
	Xiū Xī
	Massage
	按摩
	Àn Mó

Where you want to go?

Where you want to go?

	University
	大学
	Dà Xué
	Shopping Mall
	购物中心
	Gòu Wù Zhōng Xīn
	Park
	公园
	Gōng Yuán

Coffee-Shop

咖啡店

Kā Fēi Diàn

Supermarket

超市

Chāo Shì

Let's Practice

Where is park?

公园在哪?

Gōng Yuán Zài Nǎ

Where you want to go?

124

Where you want to go?

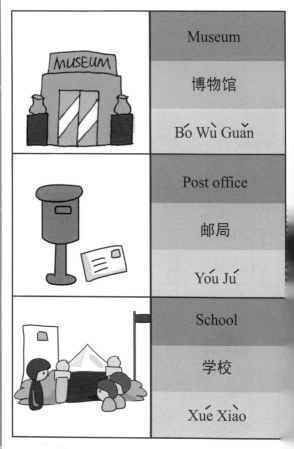

	Museum
	博物馆
	Bó Wù Guǎn
	Post office
	邮局
	Yóu Jú
	School
	学校
	Xué Xiào

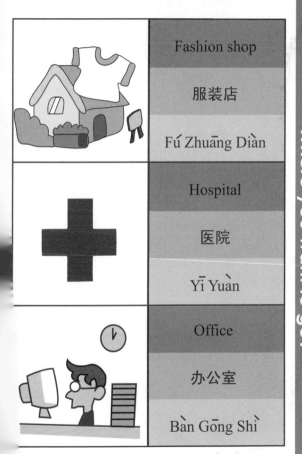

	Fashion shop
	服装店
	Fú Zhuāng Diàn
	Hospital
	医院
	Yī Yuàn
	Office
	办公室
	Bàn Gōng Shì

Where you want to go?

126

Where you want to go?

	What you want to do?
	你想做什么?
	Ni Xiǎng Zuò Shen Me?
	I want to _____
	我想_____
	Wǒ Xiǎng_____
	Play
	玩
	Wán

Where you want to go?

What you want to do?

	Speak 说 Shuō
	Smoke 吸烟 Xī Yān
	Think 想 Xiǎng

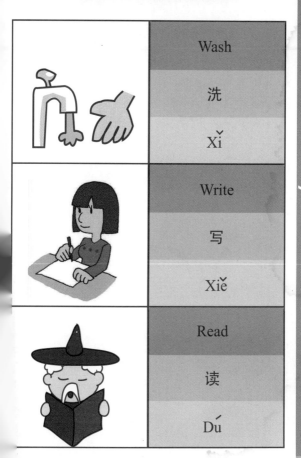

Wash

洗

Xǐ

Write

写

Xiě

Read

读

Dú

What you want to do?

What you want to do?

	Wait
	等
	Děng
	See
	看
	Kàn
	Fight
	打
	Dǎ

	Lay down
	躺
	Tǎng
	Walk
	走
	Zǒu
	Sit
	坐
	Zuò

What you want to do?

What you want to do?

	Stand
	站
	Zhàn
	Run
	跑
	Pǎo
	Change
	换
	Huàn

Conclusion

Congratulation !
You have successfully completed
Learn Chinese in 23 Minutes !

The next thing you need to do
is practice.

Now, start calling your friend or
even better buy a ticket to China.

If you come to China, please don't
forget to email me.

Author

Marcus Lee

A native Chinese speaker who is fluent in 5 Chinese dialects. Marcus has done business in 23 provinces of China. He is also the Best Selling Author of "How to Outsmart China", The Complete Guide to Successful Business in China.

Marcus was included as "The 50 Persons You Must Know in Shanghai" by Modern Weekly in 2007.

Email: drmarcus@yahoo.cn

Index

Index

Index

Index

Index

Index

Index

Index

Note

Note

Note

Note

Note

Note

Note

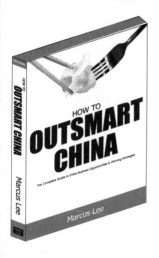

Home | Company | Services | Management | Projects | Education | Membership | Virtual office | Legal | Link | Contac

Services

Services:

Invest
Represent
Setup
Research
Training
License
Matching
Sourcing
Negotiation
Follow up
Visit
Exhibition
Advisor

Our Services

1. Co-Investment in China projects
2. Representation for foreign companies
3. Company setup, Office setup, factory setup
4. Research & Due diligence
5. Training & Seminar
6. Obtain government license
7. Business matching with our database
8. Sourcing China products
9. Assist in China Negotiation
10. Follow-up program for foreign investor
11. Accompanied visit to China
12. Exhibition Support in China

Your Gateway to China
www.chinabrm.com

Doing
Business 中国商机
in China

| Shanghai | Kuala Lumpur | London | Santiago | Los Angeles |
| 17 January 2008 | 10 February 2008 | 13 April 2008 | 20 April 2008 | 30 May 2008 |

Preview ▸   Buy ▸

Bloomberg Interview with Marcus

Bloomberg
Interview
with Marcus

Doing Business in China Seminar

★ Doing Business
in China Seminar
Course

About Marcus

About Marcus
Click here to know
more about author

…nus		
…ing Business in China Executive Seminar	Shanghai, China	3 days
…ing Business in China Seminar	Shanghai, China	3 days
…mplete China Program	Shanghai, China	7 days
…erence China Field Trip Program	Shanghai, China	4 days

…nts		
…th America Book Launch	New York, United States	29/11/2008
…ing Business in China Seminar	Santiago, Chile	21/04/2008
…ntina-China Business Forum	Buenos Aires, Argentina	28/04/2008
…dish Chamber of Commerce	Shanghai, China	01/04/2008
…sh Chamber of Commerce	Shanghai, China	14/03/2008
…Roundtable Book Launch	Kuala Lumpur, Malaysia	19/02/2008
…with Expatriate Professional Women Society	Shanghai, China	17/01/2008
…Business School (London) EMBA Briefing	London, United Kingdom	13/06/2007
…oll Business School (US) EMBA Briefing	Charlotte, North Carolina	20/05/2007

…Release		
…rview with Shanghai Star Business Journal	Shanghai, China	14/02/2008
…rview with AmericaEconomia	Santiago, Chile	29/04/2008
…rview with Bloomberg China 2008 Economic	Hong Kong SAR	02/01/2008
…al Launch of "How to Outsmart China"	Shanghai, China	06/12/2007
…d Woman Economic Forum	Abu Dhabi, UAE	18/11/2007
…ore to woes Chinese company, Bursa told	Kuala Lumpur, Malaysia	24/11/2007
…Review at Frankfurter Buch Messe	Frankfurt Main, Germany	14/10/2007
…Launch with The Star	Kuala Lumpur, Malaysia	22/11/2007

For More Information Visit:
www.outsmartchina.com

Beijing City